I'm praying that
you continue to
draw close to H[...]
always and for[...]
no matter what
you're going through.

"For I know the plans I have for you,"
declares the LORD, *"plans to prosper you*
and not to harm you, plans to give you
hope and a future."

JEREMIAH 29:11 NIV

No matter how far you feel from Him,
know that you are always welcome
to draw near. God is always there
when you seek after Him.

SOPHA RUSH

DaySpring

I'm asking God to
replace your doubts with
everlasting love and joy
and help you to see
His work in your life.

*The LORD himself goes before you
and will be with you; he will never leave you
nor forsake you. Do not be afraid;
do not be discouraged.*

DEUTERONOMY 31:8 NIV

Even when seeds of doubt try to take root,
I must not water them.
I keep His promises rooted
and engraved on my heart.

SOPHA RUSH

DaySpring

I asked God
to remind you that
He calls you
His masterpiece.

We also thank God continually because,
when you received the word of God,
which you heard from us,
you accepted it not as a human word,
but as it actually is, the word of God.

I THESSALONIANS 2:13 NIV

God is the One who will lead you
and make sure you are secure
when you feel like things are shaky.

SOPHA RUSH

When a door closes,
I'm asking God to give you
comfort in knowing it's
for your own protection.
There are things behind closed doors
we can't see, but God always has
something greater behind another.

Trust in the LORD with all your heart,
and do not lean on your own understanding.
In all your ways acknowledge him,
and he will make straight your paths.

PROVERBS 3:5-6 ESV

If there is one thing I've learned,
it's the ability to trust and
believe that God knows
what's best for me and
to stop letting doubt lead.

SOPHA RUSH

DaySpring

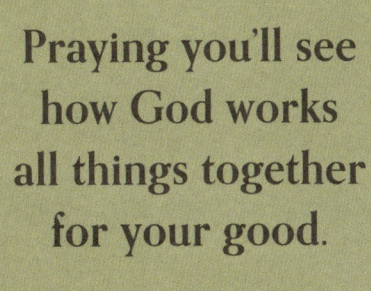

Praying you'll see
how God works
all things together
for your good.

That is why we labor and strive,
because we have put our hope
in the living God, who is the Savior
of all people.

I TIMOTHY 4:10 NIV

God is always near, walking alongside you,
leading you through your dark moments,
and shining a light on His glory.

SOPHA RUSH

DaySpring

I'm praying you'll be reminded that God will never give up on you.

The Spirit helps us in our weakness. For we do not know what to pray for as we ought, but the Spirit himself intercedes for us with groanings too deep for words.

ROMANS 8:26 ESV

God is working even when you can't see how He is about to use your pain for His purpose. The very things that were meant to destroy you actually came to build you back up stronger than ever.

SOPHA RUSH

DaySpring

I'm praying God reminds you, when you try to face your struggles alone, that you have Him, the Creator of the universe, on your side, working on your behalf and holding you through it all.

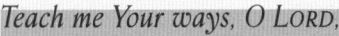

Teach me Your ways, O LORD, that I may live according to Your truth! Grant me purity of heart, so that I may honor You.

PSALM 86:11 NLT

God is always providing, down to the smallest details.

SOPHA RUSH

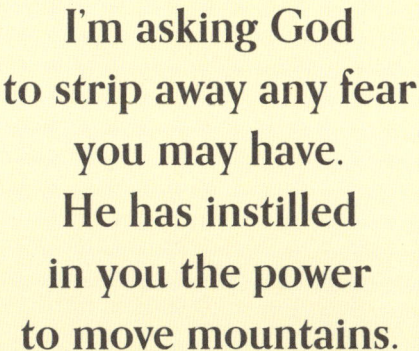

I'm asking God
to strip away any fear
you may have.
He has instilled
in you the power
to move mountains.

If the Spirit of him who raised Jesus
from the dead dwells in you,
he who raised Christ Jesus from the dead
will also give life to your mortal bodies
through his Spirit who dwells in you.

ROMANS 8:11 ESV

God has and always will be there,
every step of the way.

SOPHA RUSH

I'm asking God to give you wisdom and courage.

I lift up my eyes to the mountains—
where does my help come from?
My help comes from the LORD,
the Maker of heaven and earth.

PSALM 121:1-2 NIV

Today is an opportunity to ask God for help with any relationships that have caused you trouble, confusion, frustration, or pain. He cares about you, and He is willing to perfect those things that concern you.

SOPHA RUSH

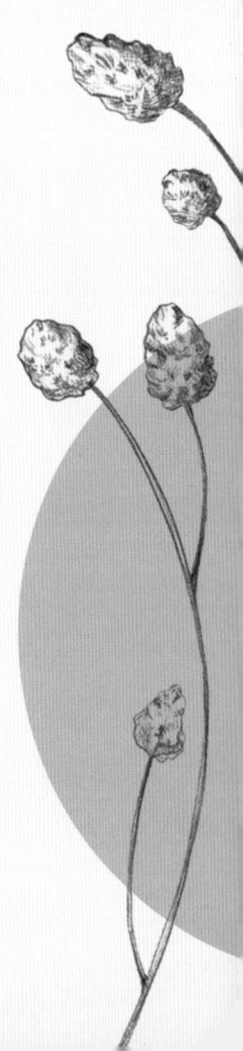

DaySpring

Today I'm asking God to help you let go of all your worries and concerns and to let Him hold you.

The Sovereign LORD has given me a well-instructed tongue, to know the word that sustains the weary. He wakens me morning by morning, wakens my ear to listen like one being instructed.

ISAIAH 50:4 NIV

Allow God to teach you the beauty of trusting Him with all your heart. He has your whole life planned and wants you to trust that He will never let you lack.

SOPHA RUSH

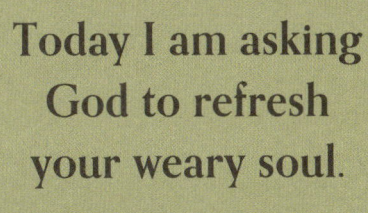

Today I am asking
God to refresh
your weary soul.

When you pray,
do not keep on babbling like pagans,
for they think they will be heard
because of their many words. Do not be like them,
for your Father knows what you need
before you ask him.

MATTHEW 6:7-8 NIV

God LOVES it when people
who know they're wrong come back to Him.

SOPHA RUSH

I'm thinking God today for His good work in and through you.

The heavens declare the glory of God; the skies proclaim the work of his hands.

PSALM 19:1 NIV

May God give you the strength to let go of anything taking up too much of your time and pulling you away from Him.

SOPHA RUSH

DaySpring

Today
I thank God
for the gift
of you!

Be joyful always, pray at all times,
be thankful in all circumstances.
This is what God wants from you in your life
in union with Christ Jesus.

1 THESSALONIANS 5:16-18 GNT

Walking with God may seem harder than
trying to find happiness and contentment
in different people and things. But I wouldn't
trade my relationship with God
for anything this world has to offer.

SOPHA RUSH

DaySpring

I'm asking God to give you peace beyond understanding as you walk through this journey.

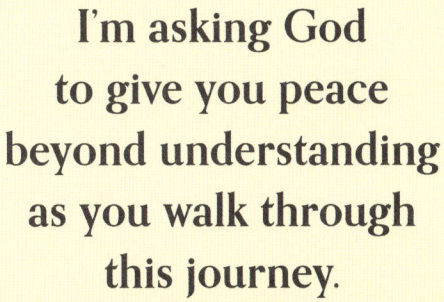

If we ask anything according to his will he hears us. And if we know that he hears us in whatever we ask, we know that we have the requests that we have asked of him.

I JOHN 5:14-15 ESV

The distractions that surround me on a daily basis will be discerned by God's truth, not by anyone else's standard for success in this life.

SOPHA RUSH

DaySpring

Today, I'm praising God for all the amazing ways He shows up in your life.

*If you abide in me,
and my words abide in you,
ask whatever you wish,
and it will be done for you.*

JOHN 15:7 ESV

God's perfect timing is everything,
and you can fully rest in Him,
knowing you have the Best
walking alongside you.

SOPHA RUSH

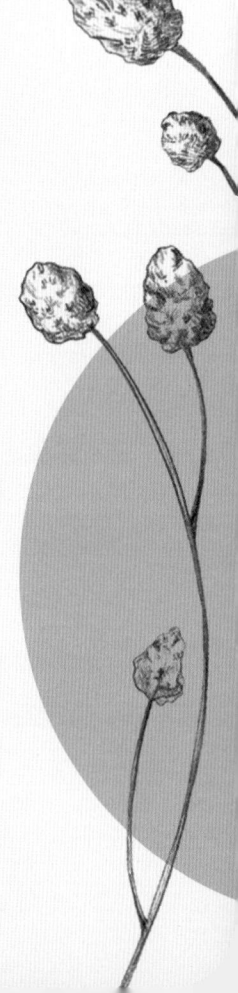

I'm praying you'll sense God's loving presence every day of your life.

I tell you, ask, and it will be given to you; seek, and you will find; knock, and it will be opened to you.

LUKE 11:9 ESV

Whether I'm washing the dishes, mentoring my girls, or just sitting in complete silence, God extends grace and teaches me in those moments.

SOPHA RUSH

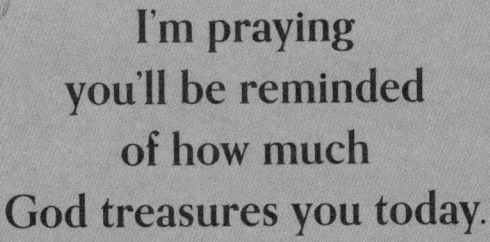

I'm praying
you'll be reminded
of how much
God treasures you today.

You are precious to me.
I give you honor,
and I love you.

ISAIAH 43:4 ICB

Your failures and struggles
are not your identity.

SOPHA RUSH

DaySpring

I'm praying God will give you peace in the midst of chaos.

Look to the LORD and his strength; seek his face always.

1 CHRONICLES 16:11 NIV

If we keep praying for God to give us the strength to seek His face every time we have a disagreement or conflict, we will be able to rely on Him to help us respond in truth and love.

SOPHA RUSH

DaySpring

I'm asking God to give you
an unwavering hope—
one that knows
He has brighter days
planned for you.

I pray that the eyes of your heart
may be enlightened in order that you may know
the hope to which he has called you.

EPHESIANS 1:18 NIV

Prayer directs us back
to the heart of God, and it changes
our perspective from what we see
to what God has in store for us.

SOPHA RUSH

DaySpring

I'm praying you'll feel God's renewal today.

*If anyone belongs to Christ,
then he is made new.
The old things have gone;
everything is made new!*

II CORINTHIANS 5:17 ICB

Each day we have been given the opportunity
to get things right with God,
because each day we have been given
a fresh start.

SOPHA RUSH

Light is coming, friend. I'm asking God to reveal His next steps for you.

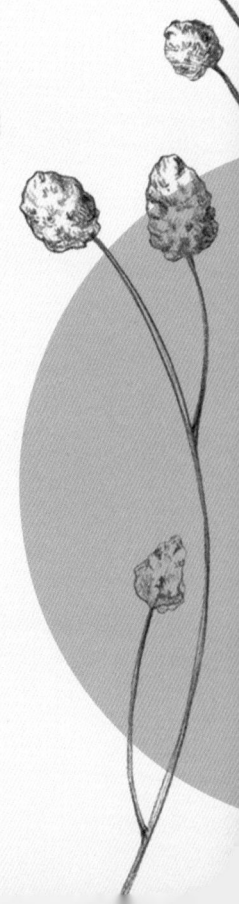

God has made us what we are.
In Christ Jesus, God made us new people
so that we would do good works.
God had planned in advance
those good works for us.
He had planned for us
to live our lives doing them.

EPHESIANS 2:10 ICB

Today I encourage you to. . . .
ask God, "What is the next best thing
You want me to do?"

SOPHA RUSH

DaySpring

I asked God to comfort you as you walk through this difficult time.

*Even if I walk through a very dark valley,
I will not be afraid because You are with me.
Your rod and Your shepherd's staff comfort me.*

PSALM 23:4 ICB

Grow through what you go through.
Because once you come out,
you will never be the same person
who walked in.

SOPHA RUSH

I'm asking the Lord
to give you the strength
you need to face all that
comes your way today.

I can do all things through Christ
because He gives me strength.

PHILIPPIANS 4:13 ICB

Rejection has happened to the best of us,
but that has never been a good reason
for us to give up.

SOPHA RUSH

DaySpring

Praying your life will be filled with pure joy and hope everlasting.

Be full of joy,
because you have
a great reward in heaven.

LUKE 6:23 ICB

Someday, when He decides to show us
the bigger picture, it will be easier
to understand the why behind
some of the things we've gone through.

SOPHA RUSH

DaySpring

I'm asking the Lord
to guide you
in this season and
all the seasons
of your life.

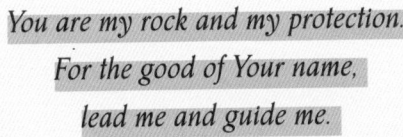

You are my rock and my protection.
For the good of Your name,
lead me and guide me.

PSALM 31:3 NCV

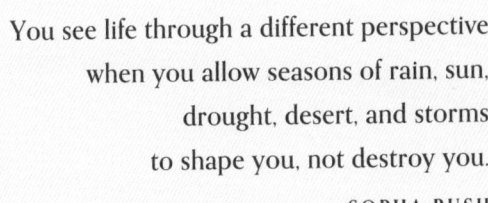

You see life through a different perspective
when you allow seasons of rain, sun,
drought, desert, and storms
to shape you, not destroy you.

SOPHA RUSH

DaySpring

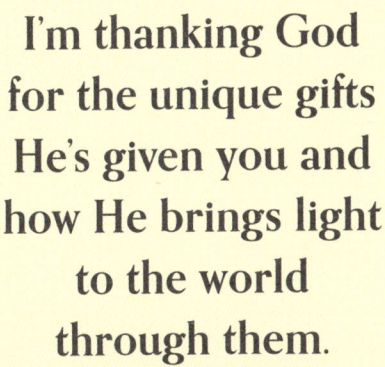

I'm thanking God for the unique gifts He's given you and how He brings light to the world through them.

*In the same way,
you should be a light for other people.
Live so that they will
see the good things you do.
Live so that they will
praise your Father in heaven.*

MATTHEW 5:16 ICB

Sometimes it's easy getting so wrapped up
in thinking that God hasn't given you
what you "need" to be successful,
but in all reality, you have more than
what you need within you.

SOPHA RUSH

DaySpring

I'm praying you'll find joy
in this season and
peace in knowing that
God is working on your behalf.

"I told you these things
so that you can have peace in Me.
In this world you will have trouble.
But be brave! I have defeated the world!"

JOHN 16:33 ICB

Keep working, keep dreaming.
Never stop using opportunities
as tools to grow.

SOPHA RUSH

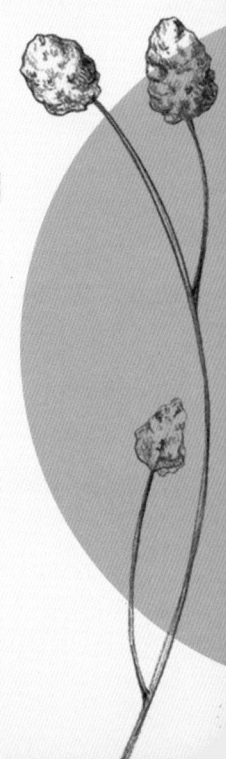

DaySpring

I'm praying that today you are able to clearly hear God's voice.

*This is love:
that we walk in obedience to his commands.
As you have heard from the beginning,
his command is that you walk in love.*

II JOHN 1:6 NIV

I can't tell you why we go
through some of the things we do,
but I can say God is in all of it
in some way, shape, or form.

SOPHA RUSH

DaySpring

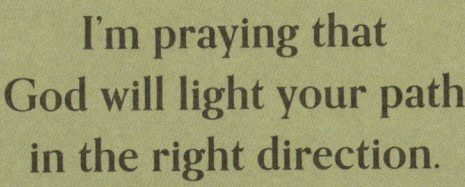

I'm praying that
God will light your path
in the right direction.

Your word is like a lamp for my feet

and a light for my way.

PSALM 119:105 ICB

Don't compromise who you are
for the sake of being liked or known.
Let your actions speak for you.
Let your obedience be what guides you.

SOPHA RUSH

I'm praying God
will remind you
of how loved you are
as He holds you
through this trying time.

Give all your worries to Him,

because He cares for you.

1 PETER 5:7 ICB

That scar you have is not the end of you.
That scar is not your identity.
That scar is a building stone,
and you are a living testimony.

SOPHA RUSH

I'm asking the Lord to reveal His bigger picture to you.

> *But seek first his kingdom*
> *and his righteousness,*
> *and all these things*
> *will be given to you as well.*

MATTHEW 6:33 NIV

God already has your blessings
named just for you.
The right doors will open
and you will never have to
force your way through.

SOPHA RUSH

I'm asking God
to help you feel
His protection at all times
and to help you release
the things that
you were never meant
to carry.

*Be wise as serpents
and innocent as doves.*

MATTHEW 10:16 ESV

Only God has the power to save.
He's a Healer, Fixer,
Protector, Restorer.
Fix your eyes on Him.

SOPHA RUSH

DaySpring

I'm praying you
enjoy the wild ride
that God has you on—
filled with wonder,
pain, hope, and
crazy experiences.

With God's power working in us,
God can do much, much more than
anything we can ask or think of.

EPHESIANS 3:20 ICB

No matter what, take care of yourself
by chasing after the dreams
God has for you. Life is too short
to worry about everyone else's journey.

SOPHA RUSH

I'm asking God to intervene in your life today. May He help you through this situation.

So don't worry, because I am with you.
Don't be afraid, because I am your God.
I will make you strong and will help you.
I will support you with my right hand
that saves you.

ISAIAH 41:10 ICB

God is able
to do more than I ask.
He exceeds
all my expectations.
SOPHA RUSH

DaySpring

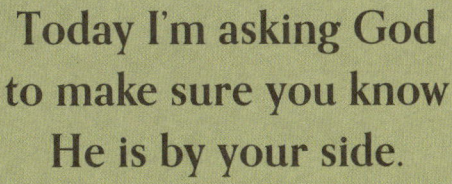

Today I'm asking God
to make sure you know
He is by your side.

The Lord defends those who suffer.
He protects them in times of trouble.
Those who know the Lord trust Him.
He will not leave those who come to Him.

PSALM 9:9-10 ICB

I want to remind you to trust in God's timing
even when things don't make sense.
Let Him take what feels like complete chaos
and have everything just fall into place.

SOPHA RUSH

DaySpring

Today
I'm thanking God
for protecting you.

*God is our protection
and our strength.
He always helps
in times of trouble.*

PSALM 46:1 ICB

You are so valuable.
Never forget it.
Even on your hard days,
the love God has for you
remains the same.

SOPHA RUSH

Today I'm praying that God breaks down every barrier in your way.

Trust the Lord with all your heart.
Don't depend on your own understanding.
Remember the Lord in everything you do.
And He will give you success.

PROVERBS 3:5-6 ICB

I could have really let life circumstances crush me and hold me back. Instead, I turned every setback into a greater comeback. I gained strength from the Lord to stay focused on what was for me, and I never looked back.

SOPHA RUSH

I'm praying you'll feel God's presence as He walks every step with you today.

You will teach me God's way to live.
Being with You will fill me with joy.
At Your right hand I will find
pleasure forever.

PSALM 16:11 ICB

God is not looking for you to perform,
He just wants you as you.

SOPHA RUSH

DaySpring

God believes in you,
even when you don't.
I'm praying
you see how talented
He has made you.

For we are God's handiwork,
created in Christ Jesus to do good works,
which God prepared in advance for us to do.

EPHESIANS 2:10 NIV

You are covered.
You are protected.
You are blessed
in Jesus' name, Amen.

SOPHA RUSH

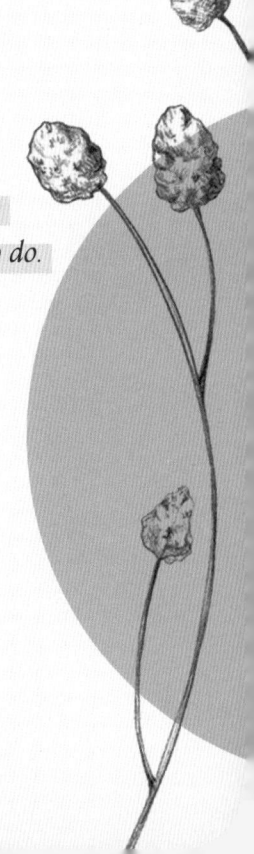

I pray
you feel God's love
toward you.

*For God so loved the world
that he gave his one and only Son,
that whoever believes in him shall not perish
but have eternal life.*

JOHN 3:16 NIV

May you be reminded to stay
focused on yourself and not
compare your journey to the next.
Everyone grows differently. Let
your garden be nurtured, your soul
bloom with gentleness.

SOPHA RUSH

DaySpring

I asked
God to refresh
your spirit today.

I will refresh the weary

and satisfy the faint.

JEREMIAH 31:25 NIV

The joy that was stripped from you will be restored.
Not only restored but resurrected with peace
that surpasses all understanding.

SOPHA RUSH

I'm praying you'll dream big dreams, knowing that nothing is impossible with God.

Jesus replied,
"What is impossible with man
is possible with God."

LUKE 18:27 NIV

Whatever you are struggling with
that is causing you to want to give up, don't.
Your comeback will be greater than ever
if you don't lose sight of the end goal
you have set for yourself.

SOPHA RUSH

DaySpring

I'm praying
you'll experience
God's presence
in your stillness.

Be still, and know that I am God;
I will be exalted among the nations,
I will be exalted in the earth.

PSALM 46:10 NIV

Nothing in your life is too messy
for Him, no failure too big. He takes
the broken and makes it beautiful,
turning ashes into beauty.

SOPHA RUSH

DaySpring

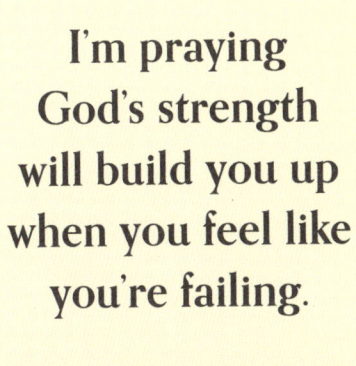

I'm praying
God's strength
will build you up
when you feel like
you're failing.

It is you who light my lamp;
the LORD my God lightens my darkness.

PSALM 18:28 ESV

God promises you,
if you trust Him with your life,
He is with you every step
of the way.

SOPHA RUSH

DaySpring

I'm asking God to continually reassure you that He has everything under control.

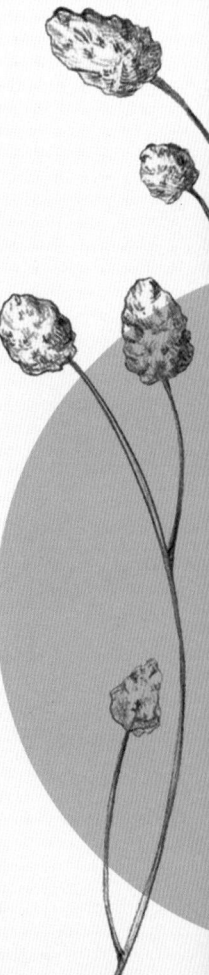

You keep him in perfect peace whose mind is stayed on you, because he trusts in you. Trust in the LORD forever, for the LORD God is an everlasting rock.

ISAIAH 26:3-4 ESV

Regardless of how crazy the path you are on seems. . . . He will continue to guide you and bless you.

SOPHA RUSH

DaySpring

I'm praying
God stays close to you
during this difficult time.

*Anyone signing up
for the kingdom of God
has to go through
plenty of hard times.*

ACTS 14:22 THE MESSAGE

Some of the best things that
have grown me and made me into
the woman I am today were the
humble beginnings, the struggles,
the failures, the setbacks.

SOPHA RUSH

DaySpring

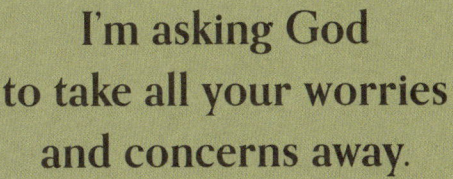

I'm asking God to take all your worries and concerns away.

Do not be anxious about anything,
but in everything by prayer and supplication
with thanksgiving let your requests
be made known to God. And the peace of God,
which surpasses all understanding,
will guard your hearts and your minds
in Christ Jesus.

PHILIPPIANS 4:6-7 ESV

Focus on what God says about worrying,
and find peace in Him alone.

SOPHA RUSH

DaySpring

I'm praying you experience joy as you wait on next steps.

*Blessed is the man
who trusts in the LORD,
whose trust is the LORD.
He is like a tree planted by water,
that sends out its roots by the stream,
and does not fear when heat comes,
for its leaves remain green.*

JEREMIAH 17:7-8 ESV

The beauty in the wait is
to know that God has something
far better than you can
even imagine.

SOPHA RUSH

DaySpring

I'm praying that God would comfort you whenever you can't catch a break.

Look to the LORD and his strength; seek his face always.

PSALM 105:4 NIV

Ask God to shed His light
on what your next steps should be.
He will always point you
in the right direction.

SOPHA RUSH

DaySpring

I'm asking God
to encourage your heart
as you continue
on your faith journey.

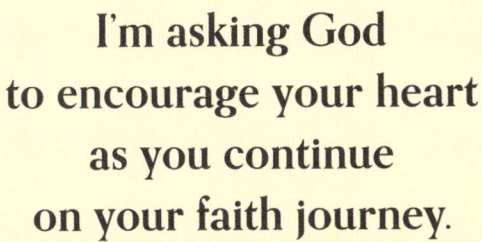

Those who know your name
trust in you, for you, LORD,
have never forsaken
those who seek you.

PSALM 9:10 NIV

May you practice quieting your mind
and sitting with God, listening more
to His voice than your own.
Ask God to renew your mind as you
begin every day relying solely on Him.

SOPHA RUSH

DaySpring

I'm asking God to meet you where you are with His comfort.

Come to me, all you who are weary and burdened, and I will give you rest.

MATTHEW 11:28 NIV

I want to encourage you, wherever you are, whatever season you are in, to understand that your calling is meant for you. No one else. Just you.

SOPHA RUSH

I'm asking the Lord
to remind you that
He will never leave you.

Let your face shine on your servant;

save me in your unfailing love.

PSALM 31:16 NIV

Trusting the process
is allowing God to build.
Even if that means starting
from the ground up.

SOPHA RUSH

DaySpring

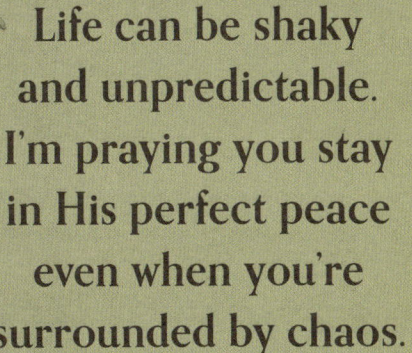

Life can be shaky
and unpredictable.
I'm praying you stay
in His perfect peace
even when you're
surrounded by chaos.

Restore us, O God;
make your face shine on us,
that we may be saved.

PSALM 80:3 NIV

I trust Him not just when it makes sense
but even when I don't understand why.

SOPHA RUSH

DaySpring

I'm praying you feel God's peace today.

Peace I leave with you;
my peace I give you.
I do not give to you as the world gives.
Do not let your hearts be troubled
and do not be afraid.

JOHN 14:27 NIV

Slow down before you miss out
on the most precious moments
in this season.

SOPHA RUSH

DaySpring

I'm praying
God will reveal
the greatness
He has for you.

You are a chosen race, a royal priesthood,
a holy nation, a people for his own possession,
that you may proclaim the excellencies of him
who called you out of darkness
into his marvelous light.

I PETER 2:9 ESV

Keep moving in obedience,
preparing for what's to come.
This is just the beginning
of something far greater.

SOPHA RUSH

DaySpring

I'm praying you'll feel God's strength and protection surround you today.

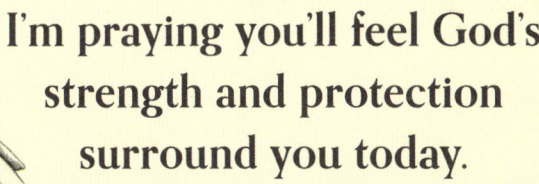

God has not given us a spirit of fear, but of power and of love and of a sound mind.

II TIMOTHY 1:7 NKJV

Everything I've endured
teaches me more about myself.
It shows me how strong I am
and how much I really need God.

SOPHA RUSH

DaySpring

I'm asking
God to send you
daily reminders of
the special gifts
He has placed
within you.

*The LORD make His face
shine upon you and
be gracious to you.*

NUMBERS 6:25 NKJV

God is the source
that keeps your fire burning.
He gives you a light
that can't be blown out.

SOPHA RUSH

DaySpring

I'm praying
you feel God's comfort
during your darkest moments.

Jesus spoke to them, saying,
"I am the light of the world.
Whoever follows me will not walk in darkness,
but will have the light of life."

JOHN 8:12 ESV

God loves you and
wants you to experience
the light within yourself.
Don't let your own thoughts
dim the very light God
has birthed in you.

SOPHA RUSH

DaySpring

I'm asking God
to dust off the dullness
in your life and to set
your soul on fire again.

You are the light of the world....
Let your light shine before others,
so that they may see your good works and
give glory to your Father who is in heaven.

MATTHEW 5:14-16 ESV

Your light that was once hidden
and buried is ready to shine like never before.

SOPHA RUSH

DaySpring

I'm praying God will remind you of how truly valuable you are.

Then the righteous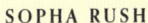
will shine like the sun
in the kingdom of their Father.

MATTHEW 13:43 NIV

However long it may take you,
just know you are worthy and valued.
Don't let anyone convince you otherwise.

SOPHA RUSH

I'm praying you feel God's power today.

Be strong in the Lord and in his mighty power.

EPHESIANS 6:10 NIV

God has said countless times how you are so loved, treasured, strong, beautiful, intelligent, wonderfully made, powerful, fearless, and enough. May you walk with your head held high, knowing that you are marked with favor.

SOPHA RUSH

DaySpring

I'm praying that
the Lord will take away
all your past pains, struggles,
and bad experiences
and replace them
with His peace.

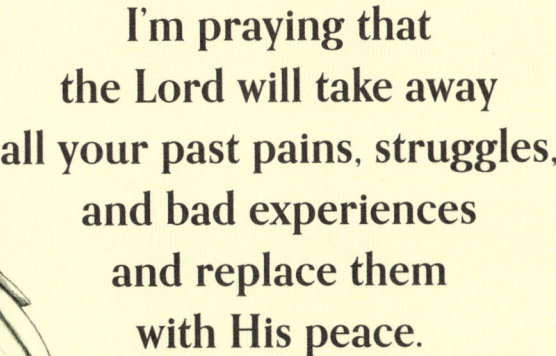

Forget the former things;
do not dwell on the past.
See, I am doing a new thing!. . . .
I am making a way in the wilderness
and streams in the wasteland.

ISAIAH 43:18-19 NIV

It's necessary to let go sometimes,
to surrender every situation to God
so it can no longer hold us captive
nor take away our peace.

SOPHA RUSH

DaySpring

I'm asking the Lord
to give you wisdom
as you make
decisions today.

The Lord *gives wisdom;*
from his mouth come
knowledge and understanding.

PROVERBS 2:6 ESV

May you receive clarity and wisdom
during the storms of your life
and cling to His goodness
and perfect truth.

SOPHA RUSH

DaySpring

I'm asking God to wrap you in love as He walks you through healing.

So do not fear, for I am with you;
do not be dismayed, for I am your God.
I will strengthen you and help you;
I will uphold you with my righteous right hand.

ISAIAH 41:10 NIV

May you truly surrender
your healing process to God
and let Him take control of it.
Freedom is calling for you.

SOPHA RUSH

DaySpring

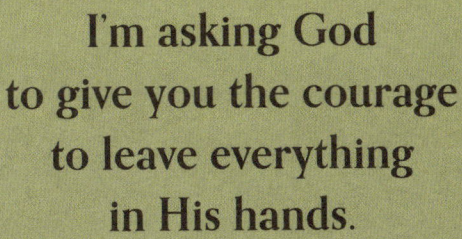

I'm asking God
to give you the courage
to leave everything
in His hands.

Cast your cares on the LORD

and he will sustain you;

he will never let the righteous

be shaken.

PSALM 55:22 NIV

When you start to feel yourself
getting overwhelmed,
take a step back. Breathe deep.
Let go of whatever you don't have control over
and leave it in His hands.

SOPHA RUSH

DaySpring

I'm asking God
to reassure you daily
that your life
is in His hands.

He who is in you is greater
than he who is in the world.

1 JOHN 4:4 ESV

You don't have to fight
whatever you're going through alone.
God has given you the strength and
power to walk in confidence.

SOPHA RUSH

DaySpring

I'm asking God to cover you completely with His grace and love.

Therefore, if anyone is in Christ, he is a new creation. The old has passed away; behold, the new has come.

II CORINTHIANS 5:17 ESV

Jesus is more powerful than any bondage that may have been handed down to you. He breaks chains and releases strongholds.

SOPHA RUSH

DaySpring

I'm asking
God to take away
all your worries today.

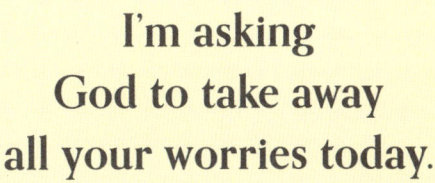

Therefore do not be anxious about tomorrow,
for tomorrow will be anxious for itself.
· Sufficient for the day is its own trouble.

MATTHEW 6:34 ESV

You can't heal
what you aren't willing to confront.

SOPHA RUSH

DaySpring

I'm asking God to complete the mending process in you, preparing you for greatness.

Now to him who is able to do far more abundantly than all that we ask or think, according to the power at work within us.

EPHESIANS 3:20 ESV

As you continually walk alongside God, may you truly rely on Him for your strength as you stay prayed up.

SOPHA RUSH

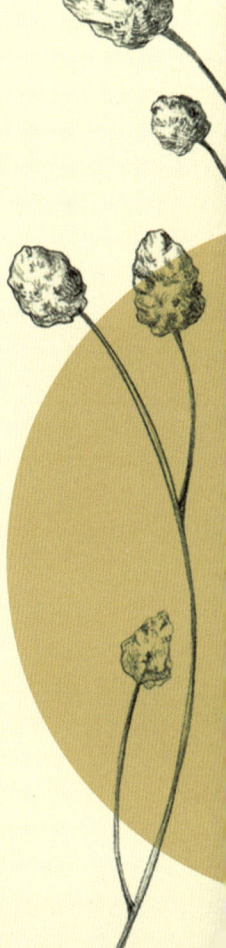

DaySpring

I'm asking God
to uproot everything
that's been stealing your joy—
the negativity, the guilt,
the shame, all of the junk
that has consumed your life.

Create in me a clean heart, O God,
and renew a right spirit within me.

PSALM 51:10 ESV

May your faith
allow you to depend
solely on God
and His provision
for your life.

SOPHA RUSH

DaySpring

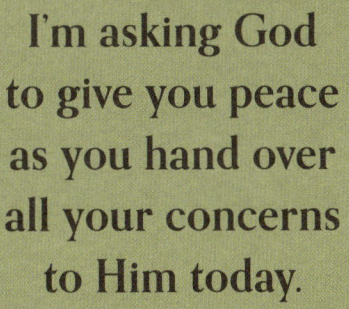

I'm asking God to give you peace as you hand over all your concerns to Him today.

The peace of God,
which surpasses all understanding,
will guard your hearts and your minds
in Christ Jesus.

PHILIPPIANS 4:7 ESV

When I give it over to God and
leave it in His hands—really leave it there—
a peace just takes over,
and His presence is evident around me.

SOPHA RUSH

DaySpring

God is your resting place. I'm praying He helps you create time to clear your mind, renew your spirit, and cleanse your heart.

Come to me,
all you who are weary and burdened,
and I will give you rest.

MATTHEW 11:28 NIV

Whatever is causing you stress,
hurt, pain, worry, fear, or uncertainty,
you can rest in the fact
that you serve a God of peace.

SOPHA RUSH

DaySpring

When you are broken
and tired and need
His rest and peace,
I'm asking God to take
all of your pain
and replace it
with His peace.

He leads me beside still waters.

He restores my soul.

PSALM 23:2-3 ESV

God wants all of you.
Every piece, broken and all.

SOPHA RUSH

DaySpring

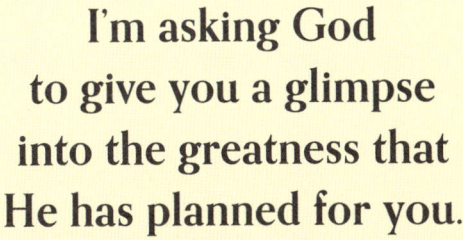

I'm asking God to give you a glimpse into the greatness that He has planned for you.

For I know the plans I have for you, declares the LORD, plans for welfare and not for evil, to give you a future and a hope.

JEREMIAH 29:11 ESV

Let God's plan for you be your main focus
and anything that isn't aligned with it
be disregarded as a tactic used
to knock you off course.

SOPHA RUSH

I'm praying that
the Lord will
restore your soul
and overwhelm you
with His peace.

*When my heart
is overwhelmed;
lead me to the rock
that is higher than I.*
PSALM 61:2 NKJV

Take some deep breaths
and be gentle with yourself.
Ask God for answers and
listen for His response.
He can lift all the heaviness.
SOPHA RUSH

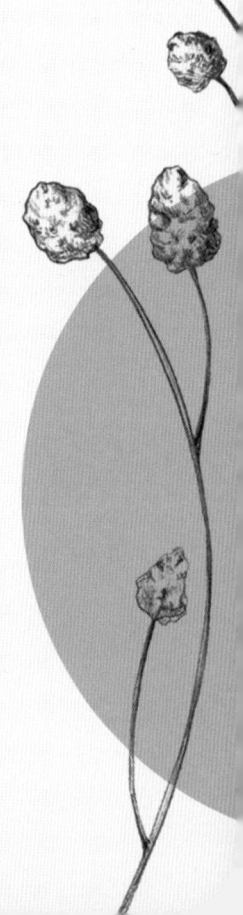

DaySpring

I'm praying you'll be reminded today that you are worthy, valuable, and treasured by God.

See what great love the Father has lavished on us, that we should be called children of God! And that is what we are!

1 JOHN 3:1 NIV

No matter what bad things you've been through—pain, struggles, abuse, bitterness— know without a doubt you are enough with God.

SOPHA RUSH

DaySpring

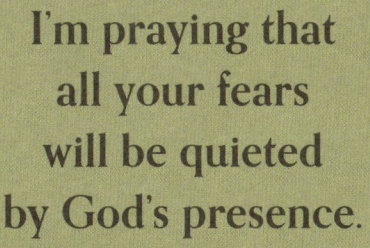

I'm praying that
all your fears
will be quieted
by God's presence.

In peace I will lie down and sleep,

for you alone, LORD,

make me dwell in safety.

PSALM 4:8 NIV

He sees you, He hears you,
He is right there with you facing giants. . . .
and overcoming strongholds.

SOPHA RUSH

I'm asking God
to give you courage
as you continue
to walk into all that
He has planned for you.

You will keep in perfect peace
those whose minds are steadfast,
because they trust in you.

ISAIAH 26:3 NIV

God is working in your life!
Look for His handiwork,
and before you know it,
you'll be pouring out love
and positivity again.

SOPHA RUSH

DaySpring

I'm praying you feel
God's presence
as you take these
first steps outside
of your comfort zone.

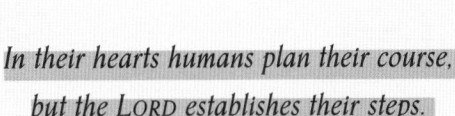

In their hearts humans plan their course,
but the Lord establishes their steps.

PROVERBS 16:9 NIV

Even when I feel like
I'm falling apart,
God is holding me together.

SOPHA RUSH

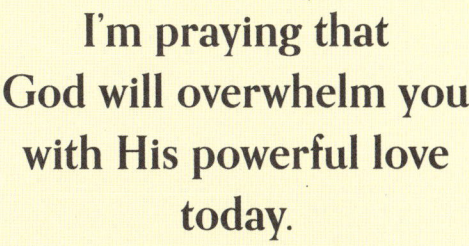

I'm praying that God will overwhelm you with His powerful love today.

Now to him who is able to do immeasurably more than all we ask or imagine, according to his power that is at work within us.

EPHESIANS 3:20 NIV

The Creator of the stars, the solar system,
the mountains, and every living being
is working on your behalf
at this very moment.

SOPHA RUSH

I'm asking God
to point you in
the right direction
today.

No eye has seen, no ear has heard,
and no mind has imagined
what God has prepared
for those who love Him.

I CORINTHIANS 2:9 NLT

God believes in you and
continues to show that in the way
He gives you favor.

SOPHA RUSH

I'm asking
God to heal
your heart today.

I love the LORD,
for he heard my voice;
he heard my cry for mercy.

PSALM 116:1 NIV

When you're down,
continue to give yourself
pep talks, fill your thoughts
with God's goodness, and remind
yourself you are a child of God.

SOPHA RUSH

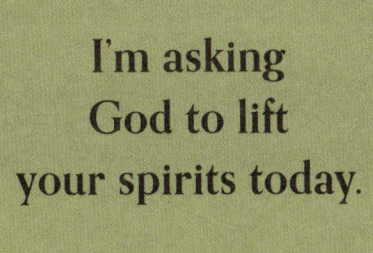

I'm asking
God to lift
your spirits today.

I have told you these things,

so that in me you may have peace.

In this world you will have trouble.

But take heart! I have overcome the world.

JOHN 16:33 NIV

My encouragement for you is to keep fighting,

keep pressing, keep persevering through the storm,

and know that your season is not in vain.

God has big things planned for you.

SOPHA RUSH

DaySpring

I'm asking
God to fill you
with His joy.

The LORD is my strength and my shield;
my heart trusts in him, and he helps me.
My heart leaps for joy,
and with my song I praise him.

PSALM 28:7 NIV

Not every day will be
pretty and full of smiles, but we know
that through Christ, we can overcome anything.
Although we may be dealing
with painful situations, we have joy
that remains in us regardless.

SOPHA RUSH

DaySpring

I'm asking God to continue to draw close to you always and forever.

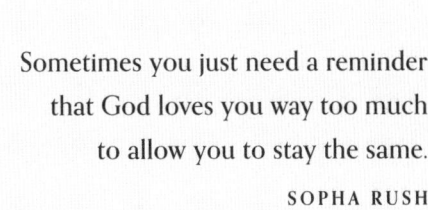

Now may the God of hope fill you with all joy and peace in believing, so that you will abound in hope by the power of the Holy Spirit.

ROMANS 15:13 NASB

Sometimes you just need a reminder that God loves you way too much to allow you to stay the same.

SOPHA RUSH

DaySpring

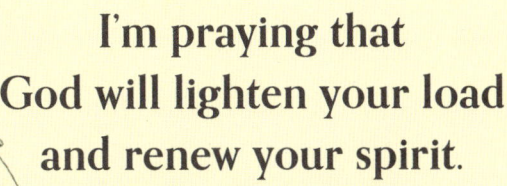

I'm praying that
God will lighten your load
and renew your spirit.

Cast all your anxiety on him

because he cares for you.

I PETER 5:7 NIV

God has the power to

soften your heart,

take away the pain,

and replace it with tenderness.

SOPHA RUSH

DaySpring

I'm asking God
to reassure you today—
He is always working
in your life.

To every thing there is a season,
and a time to every purpose
under the heaven.

ECCLESIASTES 3:1 KJV

You may not be
where you want to be,
but you are exactly
where you need to be.
No season is wasted.

SOPHA RUSH

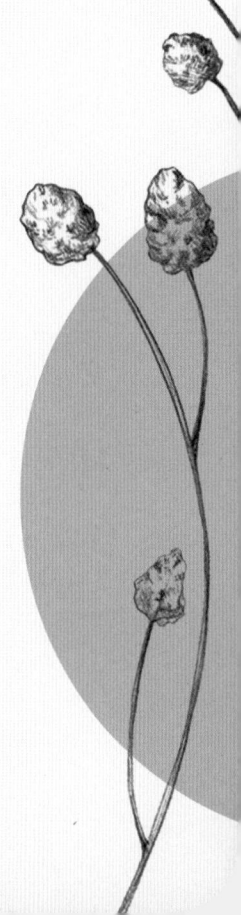

DaySpring

I'm thanking God for the gift of you today.

Let everything that has breath praise the LORD. Praise the LORD.

PSALM 150:6 NIV

I'm truly thankful for the way
He always found me.
Always rescued me.
Saving me from myself.
My light in the darkness.

SOPHA RUSH

DaySpring

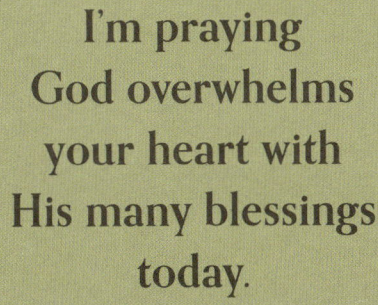

I'm praying
God overwhelms
your heart with
His many blessings
today.

Give thanks in all circumstances;
for this is the will of God
in Christ Jesus for you.

I THESSALONIANS 5:18 ESV

May your heart remain thankful
so your cup can continue
to overflow with blessings.

SOPHA RUSH

I'm praying you find
many quiet moments
when you can be still
in God's presence.
May you never be so busy
that you can't slow down and
enjoy the beauty around you.

Do not be anxious about anything,
but in everything by prayer and supplication
with thanksgiving let your requests
be made known to God.

PHILIPPIANS 4:6 ESV

The love God has for you is unmatched.
Your mistakes may have made you
feel like God couldn't love someone
like you, but don't believe that lie.
God's love for you is unconditional.

SOPHA RUSH

DaySpring

I'm praying God guides you as you face big decisions in your life.

Have faith in God. Truly, I say to you, whoever says to this mountain, "Be taken up and thrown into the sea," and does not doubt in his heart, but believes that what he says will come to pass, it will be done for him. Therefore I tell you, whatever you ask in prayer, believe that you have received it, and it will be yours.

MARK 11:22-24 ESV

God has big things planned for you. Stay focused on Him and listen for His voice.

SOPHA RUSH

DaySpring

I'm asking
God to fill you with joy
through it all.

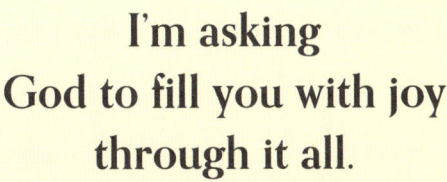

Look to the LORD and his strength;

seek his face always.

I CHRONICLES 16:11 NIV

God would never ask you
to do something that He didn't feel
you were capable of doing.
He is the strength you need to get through
whatever you are facing.

SOPHA RUSH

DaySpring

I'm praying God reminds you that nothing is impossible for Him.

And did you know that
your cousin Elizabeth conceived a son,
old as she is? Everyone called her barren,
and here she is six months pregnant!
Nothing, you see,
is impossible with God.

LUKE 1:36-38 THE MESSAGE

He is the God who does the impossible,
who calms storms, moves mountains,
and breaks generational curses.
I pray that my faithfulness will match His.

SOPHA RUSH

I'm asking God to quiet your fears and build up your confidence.

We walk by faith, not by sight.

II CORINTHIANS 5:7 ESV

When God gives you a calling and you know without a doubt that's what you're supposed to be doing, drown out the fears and renew your mind with faith.

SOPHA RUSH

I'm praying God
heals you completely today—
from all illnesses, heartaches,
and past traumas.

"But I will restore you to health
and heal your wounds,"
declares the LORD.

JEREMIAH 30:17 NIV

The temporary pain I have felt
isn't God abandoning me;
it's preparation for a lifetime of healing
and knowing I am more than a conqueror.
A warrior. A daughter of the King. In Jesus' name.

SOPHA RUSH

DaySpring

I'm praying
God's peace will fill you
as you leave your worries
in His hands.

I keep my eyes always on the LORD.
With him at my right hand,
I will not be shaken.

PSALM 16:8 NIV

Let go of whatever you don't have control over
and let Him handle it. Not just lay it down,
but actually leave it in His hands.
Let Him guide you and
protect your peace of mind.

SOPHA RUSH

I'm praying that God will take away all your negative thoughts and put your mind at ease.

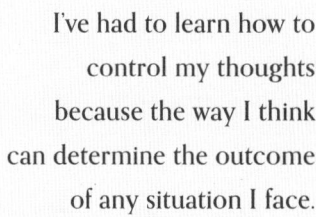

Whatever is true, whatever is noble, whatever is right, whatever is pure, whatever is lovely, whatever is admirable— if anything is excellent or praiseworthy— think about such things.

PHILIPPIANS 4:8 NIV

I've had to learn how to control my thoughts because the way I think can determine the outcome of any situation I face.

SOPHA RUSH

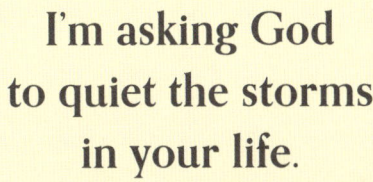

I'm asking God to quiet the storms in your life.

And when they climbed into the boat, the wind died down.

MATTHEW 14:32 NIV

Crazy how the storms in my life teach me the importance of letting go of control and letting God take care of everything like He always does.

SOPHA RUSH

I'm asking
God to let
His love overwhelm
your weary soul.

Those who hope in the LORD
will renew their strength.
They will soar on wings like eagles;
they will run and not grow weary,
they will walk and not be faint.

ISAIAH 40:31 NIV

The God you serve walks
on water, and time and time again,
He rescues, restores, and heals.
Why would He stop now? He hasn't,
and He won't. He loves you too much
not to save you.

SOPHA RUSH

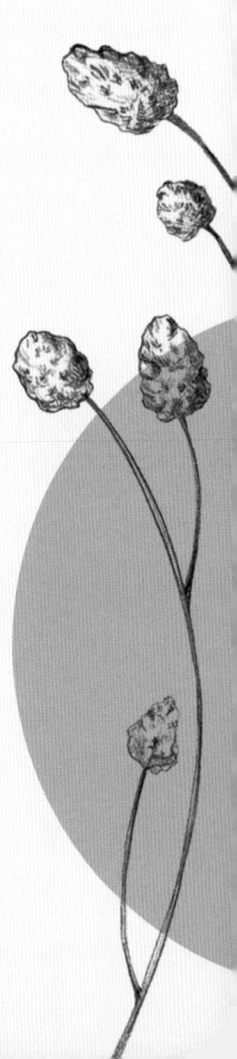

DaySpring

I'm asking God to give you
the confidence you need
to walk boldly through life,
knowing that He is always
by your side, loving you,
equipping you,
and guiding you.

*This is the confidence
we have in approaching God:
that if we ask anything according
to his will, he hears us.*

I JOHN 5:14 NIV

When you begin to live your life
in a manner pleasing to God,
you will notice the importance
of your life.

SOPHA RUSH

DaySpring